THE GUNPOWDER PLOT

By
REV. HERBERT THURSTON, S.J.

GUY FAWKES
(from a print in Pennant's London)

CATHOLIC TRUTH SOCIETY
72 VICTORIA STREET, LONDON, S.W.1
And at Liverpool, Manchester, Birmingham, Brighton,
Cardiff, Newcastle and Derby

Front cover of the Catholic Truth Society edition of 1929

THE GUNPOWDER PLOT

Rev. Herbert Thurston, S.J.

The text of this book has been taken from *The Gunpowder Plot* by Herbert Thurston, published by The Catholic Truth Society, London, 1929.

This edition published by Books Ulster in 2016.

ISBN: 978-1-910375-41-9

THE GUNPOWDER PLOT

By the Rev. Herbert Thurston, S.J.

[This account has incorporated some portions of a previous pamphlet on the same subject by the late Father John Gerard, S.J.]

Bates.   B. Winter.   C. Wright.   J. Wright.   Percy.   Fawkes.   Catesby.   T. Winter.

The gunpowder conspirators—from a print published immediately after the discovery. Taken from 'The Book of Days' (1864), edited by Robert Chambers

It is frequently asserted by certain writers that the Gunpowder Plot was the work of Catholics as a body, and was approved and countenanced by the heads of their Church, and by Catholic princes abroad.

This is quite untrue, and there is no excuse for such a statement. Whatever the plot really was, only a small handful of Catholics, thirteen in all, were found to have been concerned in it. The rest of the Catholic body not only took no part in their designs, but manifested the greatest indignation against them. As Professor Gardiner tells us (*History,* i. 264), "Their Catholic brethren spurned them from their houses"; and, as Mr. Jardine adds, "Even their own relations assailed them with threats and reproaches" (*Criminal Trials,* ii. 82). In the most recent English encyclopædia (Chambers, 1924) we read: "It is clear that the clergy in general, whether secular or regular, and the entire Catholic community, with the exception of a score of fanatics, were innocent of all participation in the plot."

That no foreign prince was engaged is proved by the emphatic testimony of the Government itself, expressed on many occasions—e.g., by Sir Edward Coke, the Attorney-General at the trial of the Conspirators.

As for the Catholic priests, only two, the Jesuits Garnet and Greenway, have been seriously accused, and it is mainly against Garnet that any attempt has been made to demonstrate a guilty complicity. His case will be more fully treated later on; at present it will be enough to say that the best Protestant historians, who have given special attention to the question, acknowledge the proofs furnished us to be insufficient to warrant a verdict against him (Jardine, *Criminal Trials,* ii. p. x.; Gardiner, *History,* i. 269, 282).

The conspirators were gentlemen of good family, who had suffered much under the iniquitous penal laws; of which the late Chief Justice Coleridge said that they were "a code as savage as any that has been conceived since the foundation of the world." This, of course, can nowise excuse the wickedness of their conspiracy. Whoever countenanced or knowingly concealed so atrocious a design was a wretch, whom no Catholic

Sir Edward Coke

would dream of defending. Should it be proved that any priest or Jesuit played so abominable a part, none would condemn him more unsparingly than his co-religionists and the brethren of his own Order, as being a scandal and disgrace to his sacred office. It is only because we believe the priests put to death on this charge to have been wholly innocent of the crime imputed to them, and to have been put to death unjustly, that we honour and defend their memory.

But although the iniquity of the penal laws does not in any way justify the conduct of the conspirators, yet, human nature being what it is, it makes it less surprising that, in so large a body as the Catholics then were, a few desperate men should be found who refused to imitate the patient submission with which the rest bore their sufferings. Misgovernment and cruelty have, in all ages, been apt to provoke violent resistance, and that a few Catholics were found to seek such a remedy proves no more than that there were men in that communion who were subject to human passions. How gross were the injuries inflicted upon them under pretence of law is fully acknowledged by Protestant writers. Mr. Jardine tells us (*Criminal Trials,* ii. 7), that the effect of the penal laws was undoubtedly "to withdraw from the Catholics the common rights and liberties of Englishmen, and to place all persons, however loyal to the existing government, who adhered from conscience and principle to the ancient religion, in a state of unmerited persecution and suffering."

The conspirators, under the influence of Catesby, their ringleader, took every precaution to conceal their design from their fellow Catholics, taking an oath not to reveal it to any one, and in particular were warned not to speak of it to any priest lest he should set himself against it. Catesby assured them that they need not mention it even in confession, as he himself could warrant them that their project, far from being sinful, was good and laudable. Catesby's servant Bates, at the time when the digging of the mine began, having shown signs of suspecting something of what was in hand, was not only required to swear secrecy, but was pressed to receive the Holy Communion in confirmation of his oath. Of this we shall have to speak further later on. Moreover, Father Garnet himself seems clearly to have understood that if the designs of the plotters had been imparted to him he would have had to take an oath of secrecy in solemn form.[1]

There is no sufficient reason to doubt the general accuracy of the Government account of the plot, so far as regards the incidents which occurred and their sequence. The leading conspirators had nearly all been concerned in earlier projects which aimed at placing the rule of the country in hands more friendly to the old religion than those of England's ministers. Robert Catesby, the ringleader, as well as Thomas Winter, John Wright, Francis Tresham, Thomas Percy, and, be it noted, Lord Monteagle, had been implicated in the crazy schemes of reform for which the Earl of Essex on the 25th February, 1601, had paid the forfeit with his life. In 1602 Winter had gone to Spain to solicit foreign support for his fellow Catholics, in view of the crisis which was deemed likely to occur as soon as the Queen died. This appeal had met with no material response, though Sir Edward Coke declared at the trial of the conspirators that Winter returned laden with hopes and with the promise of the Spanish King to send an army into Milford Haven and to contribute to the enterprise 100,000 crowns. Meanwhile Percy had been employed in a particular mission to Scotland, and there is good reason to believe that he did obtain from King James a promise of toleration for Catholics in the event of his succeeding to the English throne. No disturbance took place when, on Elizabeth's death, James made his way to London. So cordial was

---

[1] See J. H. Pollen in *The Month*, May, 1888, p. 67, note 18.

the attitude of his new subjects that he laid aside all his misgivings. "Na, na," he was heard to say, "we'll not need the Papists noo." In point of fact, after the collapse of Watson's Plot, which was revealed by the Catholics themselves, the recusancy fines and other penalties were remitted for a short period. But the Puritan faction were ill-pleased at this remissness. Money was needed, for the King's Scottish followers were rapacious, while the Pope was seemingly unwilling to gratify James in coercing English Catholics suspected of disloyalty. Accordingly, on the 22nd February, 1604, a proclamation was issued providing for the banishment of Catholic priests, which was followed in July by an Act of Parliament confirming all the Elizabethan statutes against recusants, and towards the end of the same year measures were taken in earnest to exact from wealthy Papists the payment of the old ruinous fines. In the interval, the hotheads of the party, seeing that James's promises of toleration could not be trusted, hatched the plot which was to be so famous in history. As early as March, 1604, Catesby seems to have conceived the main idea of using gunpowder to destroy the whole executive of the country at one blow, and then to have imparted his scheme to Percy and Thomas Winter. Winter raised some objections, and it was possibly in the hope of finding a less desperate solution of the difficulty that he went over to Flanders in April and tried to secure for the benefit of English Catholics the intervention of the Constable of Castile. In that quarter, however, he obtained nothing but vague promises, so that, reverting to Catesby's scheme of violence, he imparted some inkling of the design to a resolute Yorkshireman, one Guy Fawkes, who had taken service with the Spanish army in the Netherlands. Fawkes returned with him to England, and in May, 1604, the five first conspirators, Catesby, Thomas Winter, Percy, John Wright, and Fawkes, met at a house behind St. Clement's Inn and took an oath of secrecy. Mass was then said in an adjoining room, at

King James I

which they communicated together, but the priest—erroneously believed by some of them to be the Father John Gerard who, a few years before, had escaped from the Tower—knew nothing of their secret. In fact, as already mentioned, Catesby was urgent that nothing should be said to the priests, even in confession. On May 24th an agreement was signed for the lease of part of Whynniard's block of buildings, abutting on the Parliament House, but a Government Committee claimed the right of sitting there, and the further proceedings of the conspirators in that direction had to be postponed.

In the meantime, however, they busied themselves about accumulating a store of powder, and shortly before Midsummer, 1604, Robert Keyes was sworn in to take charge of the house in Lambeth where they collected it. When the Parliament was prorogued on July 7th, it was understood that the next session would open in the following February. The conspirators consequently set to work with a will as soon as they obtained unimpeded use of their Westminster lodging. Their design was to drive a mine under the Parliament House, and for this they found it necessary to enrol one or two new recruits. Catesby's servant, Bates, who was thought to suspect something of their design, was for precaution's sake required to take the oath, but he never worked at the mine. John Grant, Christopher Wright, and Robert Winter, the two latter being brothers of the conspirators already named, were only admitted in January. The plotters seem to have taken precautions not to be seen going in and out of their tenement. They laid in provisions as for a siege, and went on stealthily digging and tunnelling, while the only one who showed himself in public was Fawkes, a man little known in London. Moreover, to avert suspicion, Fawkes now called himself Johnson, and pretended to be the servant of Percy, in whose name the house had been hired. Percy, a connection of the Earl of Northumberland, for whom he acted as confidential steward, had some sort of official connection with Westminster.

The mining operations proved much more difficult than was anticipated, the walls of the Parliament House being as much as 9 feet thick. They made very slow progress therefore, and it

The vault beneath the old House of Lords—from an original drawing.
Taken from 'The Book of Days' (1864), edited by Robert Chambers

must have been good news to most of them when they heard
that Parliament had been further prorogued and would not meet
until October. They continued their operations after Christmas,
but now with less haste, and meanwhile accident disclosed the
fact that it was possible to hire the cellar immediately under
the Lords' Chamber. The previous tenant had stored coals there
and was disposing of his stock. Accordingly, forsaking the mine,
they concentrated their efforts upon the cellar, bringing their
powder into it by night and covering the barrels with faggots
and lumber. It was seemingly not before June 9th, 1605, when
the practical consequences of these preparations began to stare
them in the face, that Catesby, finding it necessary to allay the

scruples of some of the plotters, approached Father Garnet, the Jesuit Provincial, and put to him a suppositious case, upon which more will be said later. He professed to have obtained an answer which might set their consciences at rest. Meanwhile their plans took more definite form. It was decided that when the government of the country had been paralysed by the destruction at one blow of King, Lords, and Commons, the conspirators were to surprise the person of the Princess Elizabeth, James I's daughter, issue a proclamation in her name, and make themselves masters of the Tower, with other strongholds. As this would involve the acquisition of arms and horses, more money was needed, and three wealthy men—Ambrose Rookwood, Sir Everard Digby, and Francis Tresham—were induced to join the plot, taking, of course, the same oath of secrecy as the rest. Additional time was afforded for concerting their plans by the further postponement of the meeting of Parliament until November the 5th. What precise measures were contemplated for securing the absence from the assembly of certain catholic-ly-minded peers we do not know. There can be little doubt that some effort would have been made to save them. But on October 26th a mysterious communication was brought to Lord Monteagle, the brother-in-law of Francis Tresham. Its exact terms—the original document is still in existence—were as follows:

> "my lord out of the love i heave to some of youer friends i have a caer of youer preservacion therefor i would advyse yowe as yowe tender youer lyf to devyse some exscuse to shift of youer attendance at this parleament for god and man hath concurred to punishe the wickednes of this tyme and thinke not slightlye of this advertisement but retyere youre self into your countri wheare yowe maye expect the event in safti for thowghe theare be no apparance of anni stir yet i

saye they shall receyve a terribel blowe this parleament and yet they shall not seie who hurts them this cowncel is not to be contemned because it may do yowe good and can do yowe no harme for the danger is passed as soon as yowe have burnt the letter and i hope god will give yowe the grace to mak good use of it to whose holy protection i comend yowe."

The letter was taken to the virtual Prime Minister, Robert Cecil, by this time created Earl of Salisbury, who professed to think it the effusion of a lunatic, but, nevertheless, made it his duty on November 3rd to show it to the King. According to the official account of the plot, as subsequently published, James, under the direct guidance of Heaven, was the first to discern the true meaning of the mysterious phrase, "the danger is passed as soon as you have burnt this letter." It imported that an attempt was to be made by an act as instantaneous as the burning of a scrap of paper—in other words, by an explosion of gunpowder. It was decided then to search the cellar under the Parliament House, but to take no steps until the last moment. The Earl of Suffolk, as Lord Chamberlain, making pretext of a search for certain property which was in Whynniard's keeping, visited the cellar about 3 p.m. on November 4th. The door was opened by Fawkes, who said he was Percy's servant and that the pile of coals and faggots belonged to his master. A second visit was paid just before midnight. Fawkes, who was still there, was now arrested, having in his possession a dark lantern and materials for making a slow match to ignite the powder. Further, on removing the faggots, the vast accumulation of explosives was plainly made visible.

In the meantime news of the mysterious letter had been conveyed to the conspirators. Monteagle, on receiving it, had handed it to a gentleman in his service, one Thomas Ward, to read aloud at table to all who were then with him, and Ward,

Portrait of Robert Cecil, 1st Earl of Salisbury, circa 1608

who was a Catholic, had communicated the general drift to Thomas Winter. S. R. Gardiner is of opinion not only that Francis Tresham was responsible for the sending of the letter, but that the whole plan of discovery had been thought out between him and Monteagle in such a way that, on the one hand, the intended catastrophe might be frustrated, and, on the other, the conspirators might have time to make good their escape. Jardine is prepared to go even further. Many considerations, he says, tend to confirm the opinion expressed by Father Greenway in his narrative that the particulars of the plot had been fully revealed to Lord Salisbury by Monteagle, and that the letter was a mere contrivance of the Government to conceal the means by which their information had really been obtained.

Unfortunately, Catesby and the others were still resolute in their former purpose. They hoped that no importance would be attached to the mysterious warning, for Tresham, when charged on November 1st with betraying the plot, swore that he was unjustly suspected. Still Tresham asserted the next day that Salisbury knew what was going on, and urged them again to fly, supplying £100 in cash. Catesby seems then to have weakened, but, Percy and the others persisting in the design, Fawkes, with a courage worthy of a better cause, undertook to go through with the plan as arranged. It was not until after his arrest in the cellar that the leading conspirators in the early hours of November 5th rode out of London at full gallop, making for the rendezvous, namely the hunting party organised by Sir Everard Digby at Dunchurch near Rugby, where the conspirators, if all had gone well, had hoped to get possession of the Princess Elizabeth, then at Coventry, not far off. Catesby reached his mother's house at Ashby St. Legers, about ten miles from Dunchurch, that evening, and was soon in communication with those who had mustered in the neighbourhood. As the tidings of failure leaked out, many there assembled, seeing that further efforts were hopeless, dispersed in all haste. Those most deeply committed made their way westwards with such arms and horses as they could seize by force, riding first to Robert Wright's house at Huddington, which they reached on the afternoon of Wednesday, November 6th, and thence to Holbeche in Staffordshire, the home of Stephen Littleton. It was here, on Friday, November 8th, that they were surrounded and fired upon by the Sheriff of Worcestershire. Catesby, Percy, and the two Wrights were killed. Thomas Winter and Rookwood, who were both wounded, were taken prisoners, and with them another conspirator, Grant. Sir Everard Digby had left the company early that morning, but fell into the hands of his pursuers later in the day. Tresham was arrested in London on November 12th, and Bates about the same time in Staffordshire, but Robert Winter, with Stephen Littleton, eluded capture for two months. It was only on January 9th that they were finally betrayed at Hagley in Worcestershire. The conspirators were tried in Westminster Hall on January 27th, and were executed in two batches on January 30th and 31st.

When, after repeated examinations, in which torture, at least occasionally, played its part, the eight prisoners were arraigned, they all pleaded not guilty; not, as Lingard explains, "because they denied their participation in the conspiracy, but because the indictment contained much to which, till that day, they had been strangers. It was false that the three Jesuits had been the authors of the conspiracy, or had ever held consultations with them on the subject: as far as had come to their knowledge, all three were innocent."[1] As for their own general attitude in this solemn hour, it may be summed up in the words of the same careful historian:

---

[1] Lingard *History of England* (Ed. 1859), Vol. III., pp. 70-1.

The Death of Catesby, from 'Guy Fawkes: or, the Gunpowder Treason' by William Harrison Ainsworth, illustrated by George Cruikshank

"With respect to themselves, they had certainly entertained the design laid to their charge; but, whatever men might think of the fact, they would maintain that their intention was innocent before God. Some of them had already lost most of their property—all had suffered severely on account of their religion. The King had broken his promise of toleration, and the malice of their enemies daily aggravated their burdens. No means of liberation was left but that which they had adopted. Their only object was to relieve themselves and their brethren from the cruelty of the persecutors, and to restore a worship which in their consciences they believed to be the true worship of Christ; and for this they had risked, and for this they were ready to sacrifice, their fortunes and lives."

So much for the tragic history and sad fate of the lay conspirators. They were men who admitted their guilt, recognised the inevitableness of the penalty they paid, and showed themselves in the end conscience-stricken for the odium and the aggravation of suffering they had brought upon their fellow Catholics. But we must pass on now to consider the case of the priests, all of them Jesuits, whom the Government sought to implicate in the same conspiracy. The evidence against them was of a very different kind, and, though two of them perished on the scaffold, they denied from first to last not only in their public examinations, but in private correspondence which the writers believed to be secure from interference, any sympathy with, or complicity in, the measures of violence which the plotters had devised.

It is in connection with Father Greenway (his true name seems to have been Tesimond, but the other is more generally used by writers on the subject) that the question of the complicity of the Jesuits primarily arises. Both Jardine and Gardiner call attention to the fact that the priests were first implicated by the deposition of Thomas Bates, Catesby's servant, who was examined, probably under torture, or threat of torture, on December 4th, 1605. True, Guy Fawkes on November 9th had stated that Father John Gerard—we mean, of course, the elder John

Gerard, who was a missionary in England at the beginning of the seventeenth century—said Mass and gave Communion to the conspirators on the occasion when they first bound themselves to their nefarious purpose by an oath of secrecy. But Fawkes expressly added that the said Father "knew not their purpose," a qualification which Sir Edward Coke shamelessly suppressed when he quoted this evidence in Court. In fact, Dr. Gardiner himself states: "My own opinion is that Gerard was innocent of any knowledge of the plot."[1] Moreover, we possess the copy of a letter which was written on December 4th by Cecil, then Earl of Salisbury and virtual Prime Minister, to one Favat, who was to communicate its contents to the King. "Most of the prisoners," writes Cecil, "have wilfully forsworn that the priests knew anything in particular and obstinately refuse to be accusers of them, yea, what torture soever they be put to."

At the same time it is plain that something had just then happened which gave Cecil hopes of being able to implicate the Jesuits as fully as the King could desire, for he goes on:

> "You may tell His Majesty that if he please to read privately what this day we have drawn from a voluntary and penitent examination, the point, I am persuaded (but I am no undertaker), shall be so well cleared, if he forbear to speak much of this but a few days, as we shall see all fall out to the end whereat His Majesty shooteth."[2]

We can have little doubt that the expectation of further revelations compromising the Jesuits had been suggested to Cecil's mind by the disclosures which Bates had made when under examination that very day (December 4th). What was

---

[1] *What Gunpowder Plot Was*, p. 177.

[2] MS. Add. 6178, fol. 98, in the British Museum.

it Bates had said? We do not possess the original minute which was presumably taken down at the time, and witnessed by the Lords Commissioners whose names are appended in the copy. The copy, however, which we have was apparently produced in court in the presence of the Commissioners who had assisted at the examination, and Dr. Gardiner rightly argues that to make any material alteration in a document which was witnessed by seven leading peers would have been a rather audacious proceeding even in those days of irregular justice. Assuming, then, for the nonce that the copy of the examination of December 4th is trustworthy, what do we find?

Bates begins by explaining that Catesby had sent him to hire a lodging close by the Parliament House; but, perceiving in course of time that he suspected something, Winter and his master had made known to him that they were concerned in a dangerous matter connected with that edifice, and induced him to take an oath of secrecy which was to be confirmed by the reception of Holy Communion. For this purpose Bates had first made his confession to Father Greenway, or, to quote more exactly the terms of the deposition itself, they (i.e., Catesby and Thomas Winter)

> made this examinate take an oath to be secret in the business, which being taken by him, they told him that it was true that they meant to do somewhat about the Parliament House, namely, to lay powder under it to blow it up. Then they told him that he was to receive the Sacrament for the more assurance; that thereupon he confessed to Greenway, and told him he was to conceal a very dangerous piece of work that his master and Thomas Winter had imparted to him; and that he, being fearful of it, asked the counsel of Greenway, telling the said Greenway (which he was not desirous to hear) their particular intent and purpose of blowing up

the Parliament House; and Greenway, the priest, thereunto said that he would take no notice thereof, but that he (Bates) should be secret in what his master had imparted to him, because that was for a good cause, and that he willed this examinate to tell no other priest of it; saying moreover, that it was not dangerous unto him, nor any offence to conceal it; and thereupon Greenway gave him absolution and he received the Sacrament in company of his master and Mr. Thomas Winter.

Though the reports we possess of the trials both of the lay conspirators on January 27th and of Father Garnet on March 28th are very imperfect and unsatisfactory, it is clear from the Government statement, published in *A True and Perfect Relation,* that on both occasions Sir Edward Coke, the Attorney-General, made very great use of this deposition of the witness Bates. The object which beyond all others the prosecution had at heart was to implicate the priests, for if their complicity in such a dastardly attempt to exterminate King, Lords, and Commons could be clearly established, the policy proscribing all Romanist ecclesiastics would be justified in the eyes of the whole world. Coke accordingly narrated on January 27th how, when Bates made his confession to Father Greenway and manifested some scruple regarding the lawfulness of such a design, Greenway encouraged him to proceed. That at least was the impression which Coke sought to produce, keeping, on the whole, pretty close to the terms of the deposition, but inserting his own interpretations here and there, as even the published account enables us to see.[1] Coke's words, according to the report printed in *A True and Perfect Relation,* ran thus:

---

[1] Of course, the audience whom Coke addressed had not before them, as we have, the precise terms of Bates's deposition, attested by the seven Lords Commissioners.

"Then did they [i.e., Catesby and Winter] make Bates take an oath to be secret in the action, which being taken by him, they then told him that it was true that they were to execute a great matter, namely, to lay powder under the Parliament House to blow it up. Then they also told him that he was to receive the Sacrament for the more assurance, and thereupon he went to confession to the said Tesimond [i.e., Greenway] the Jesuit, and in his confession told him that he was to conceal a very dangerous piece of work that his master Catesby and Thomas Winter had imparted unto him, and said he much feared (the matter to be utterly unlawful), and therefore therein desired the counsel of the Jesuit, and revealed unto him the whole intent and purpose of blowing up Parliament House (upon the first day of the Assembly, at what time the King, the Queen, the Prince, the Lords spiritual and temporal, the Judges, the Knights, citizens, and burgesses, should all have been there convented and met together). But the Jesuit (being a confederate therein before, resolved and encouraged him in the action), and said that he should be secret in that which his master had imparted unto him, for that it was for a good cause. Adding moreover that it was not dangerous unto him nor any offence to conceal it. And thereupon the Jesuit gave him absolution and Bates received the Sacrament of him in the company of his master Robert Catesby and Thomas Winter."[1]

Anyone who compares the text of the examination of Bates with Coke's report of it will see that the agreement even in the minute details of the wording is in general very close. On the other hand, Coke has made certain additions, which I have indicated by enclosing them in round brackets. There is not

---

[1] *A True and Perfect Relation,* Signature G. 2.

a word in Bates's deposition which implies that the explosion was to take place when the King, Lords, and Commons were assembled, neither does Bates declare that "the Jesuit was a confederate therein before," neither does he say that "he resolved and encouraged him in the action." Moreover, there is a quite remarkable restraint in Coke's reference to the clause "that he (Bates) should be secret in that which his master had imparted unto him, because that was for a good cause." Knowing, as we do, the Attorney-General's normal violence, one would have expected an outburst here upon the monstrous impiety of the suggestion that the murder of the King and all his counsellors was for a good cause. Why does Coke refrain? It was, we believe, because he knew—and because the Lords Salisbury, Northampton, Nottingham, Suffolk, and Worcester, there present, who had attested Bates's deposition, also knew—that Bates had never heard from Greenway any commendation of the design itself. The priest had never said that the blowing up of the Parliament House was for a good cause. What Greenway had been asked by Bates was whether he might keep his master's secret. To this question he had answered Yes, and he had added that not only was such silence for a good cause, but that Bates ought "to tell no other priest of it." When we read the deposition again in the light of this suggestion, the whole statement is seen to hang together. Bates was simply Catesby's faithful servant. He was not regarded by the conspirators themselves as participating in the plot. His name is not included in the list of confederates given by Fawkes on November 17th. They knew he could not be blind to what was going on. They induced him to take an oath of secrecy about it, but his conscience was uneasy regarding this promise of silence, and he mentioned it in confession. Greenway reassured him, and told him that to conceal it was not wrong—indeed that he ought not to speak of it to anyone, not even to a priest. Why did he give such advice? Certainly not because he hoped to see the conspirators' purpose realised, but because he foresaw the terrible consequences to the Catholic cause if the plot became known. All the penal laws would be enforced with renewed severity. There would be endless arrests and cruel torture of those suspected. Capital would be made out of the discovery to inflame anti-Catholic feeling throughout the kingdom. On the other hand, there was good reason to hope that, if matters were kept quiet, the project would never go further. The mine itself—at this date, December, 1604, there was no thought of hiring the cellar—was already presenting many unforeseen difficulties. Strong prohibitions were looked for from Rome, which Greenway doubtless thought might prove an efficacious deterrent. Spain showed no disposition to lend substantial support to any uprising of English Catholics. Under such circumstances, so Greenway must have calculated, the conspirators would not long persist in such a crazy scheme. As long as any hope remained of frustrating the plot by peaceful persuasion, it would be an outrage to betray these much enduring men who were their fellows and their benefactors but at the same time the victims of a misguided zeal. To save them was "a good cause," but one that demanded the strictest secrecy about what had been projected.

But, more than this, there is every reason to suppose that Greenway did not at the time grasp what was really intended. To us now who have been at least vaguely familiar from childhood with the story of Gunpowder Treason, it appears plain that a mine under the Parliament House could have had no other motive than the destruction of those who sat in the national assembly. The very form of Bates's statement—"they told him it was true that they meant to do somewhat about the Parliament House, namely, to lay powder under it to blow it up"—suggests that their purpose was not then so clear to him and Greenway. It is, when one thinks of it, highly improbable that Catesby and Winter would have revealed to Bates their whole design. They might, for all the servant then knew, have meant no more than to destroy the material building as an act of terrorism and a signal for revolt, just as they might for a similar purpose have tried to blow up old St. Paul's or London Bridge. Greenway, on Bates's own showing, was not anxious to learn particulars. The one point he was clear about was that Bates was at that time justified in keeping his master's secret. Moreover, there is strong evidence that Bates, servant though he was, did not participate in the mining operations. Fawkes expressly declared that "all seven" who worked at the mine, "were gentlemen by name and blood, and not one was employed about this action (no, not so much as in digging and mining) that was not a gentleman."[1] Such heavy manual labour was pre-eminently a servant's work; there must have been some good reason why Bates did not share in it. May it not be that Greenway, while justifying Bates in keeping his master's secret in view of the terrible consequences which disclosure might bring both upon himself[2] and the whole Catholic body, was urgent that he should not directly co-operate in an undertaking which he suspected to be morally indefensible. It is also perhaps worth notice that Greenway had apparently had his mind directed to the material damage which would be caused by an explosion underneath the Parliament House, for he speaks in his narrative of "the very serious loss which would result from the destruction of these ancient and most imposing buildings and the perishing of the archives and papers of the Court."[3]

---

[1] Fawkes's Examination of November 8th. These words seem expressly intended to exonerate Bates.

[2] No scruple was at this date felt about torturing "those of the inferior sort" when information was wanted or hoped for.

[3] Greenway MS., fol. 68.

The most curious feature in Bates's case is a letter written by him shortly before his execution, and preserved to us in the narrative of Gerard the elder.[1] In this Catesby's servant shows himself scrupulously anxious to be honest in money matters, just as he had apparently been scrupulous about the question of keeping his master's secret. But, while in that letter he accuses himself of weakness, owns to having said that he saw "them all" (apparently the Jesuit Fathers Greenway, Gerard, and Garnet) together with Catesby at Harrowden, Lord Vaux's house, and admits that he had fetched Greenway from Father Garnet at Coughton, to come to Huddington to meet Catesby on the morrow of the discovery of the plot, he makes no reference whatever to his examination of December 4th. One would infer that he had no consciousness of having on that occasion given anything away, although, as we have seen, his deposition of December 4th appears to state that Greenway told him that the outrage they were contemplating was for a good cause and that he ought consequently to do as his master told him. If Bates had really said or implied on December 4th that Greenway in confession had expressed approval of the plot, it is difficult to understand how this honest serving-man, with death before his eyes, could have failed to reproach himself deeply for such a betrayal, even had the fact itself been true. If, however, he had only made known that Greenway in confession told him that he ought to keep his master's secret, that was quite a different matter and called for no remorse.

The importance of the witness, Thomas Bates, in the history of the Gunpowder Plot, has been to a large extent lost sight of, owing, no doubt, to his menial position. But it is certain that it was he who, by mentioning Father Greenway

---

[1] The letter is printed in full in Morris, *The Condition of Catholics under James I.,* pp. 210-211.

when under examination on December 4th, 1605, first gave the Government hope of implicating the priests, and it is equally certain that his second deposition—on January 13th, 1606, in which Greenway and Garnet were named as consorting with, and rendering service to, some of the leading conspirators—led two days later to the issue of the proclamation denouncing the Jesuits concerned and promising rewards for their apprehension. With the shameless disregard of truth which was usual in such circumstances, the proclamation declared it to be "evident" that three Jesuit Fathers—Garnet, Gerard and Greenway— were all proved guilty of the plot "by divers confessions of many conspirators." What these divers confessions of many conspirators were, the Government were careful never to reveal. No trace of them has been discovered among the copious documents which are still preserved in the Public Record Office and at Hatfield. Neither were they cited by Sir Edward Coke at either of the trials. There seems at the date of the Proclamation (January 15th) to have been absolutely nothing which tended to implicate the Jesuits except the depositions of Bates just referred to and the statement of Guy Fawkes that the conspirators, after taking the oath, received Communion from Father Gerard, who, as Fawkes's written examination bears witness, "was not acquainted with their purpose." But this clause, as noted above, by Coke's express direction was not read out in court. The proclamation, however, having once been issued, a vigorous search began, and a fortnight later, on the same day on which the first company of conspirators was executed, the hiding-place where Fathers Garnet and Oldcorne (alias Hall) had secreted themselves was discovered at Hendlip Hall. They were so stiff and weak from want of food and their cramped position that they could not extricate themselves without assistance. Let it be sufficient to say here that no attempt was made to produce evidence implicating Father Oldcorne directly in the plot. He was brought to London with Garnet, was tortured in the hope of obtaining further information, but without result, and he finally was tried and executed at Worcester, the main charge against him being that he had aided and abetted Garnet in his attempt to escape. Still more tragic was the fate of the Jesuit lay-brother, Nicholas Owen, also captured at Hendlip. He had been racked by Topcliffe, the priest-hunter, in 1594. He was now again tortured for seven hours, but nothing could be extracted from him. The next day he was found dead, and the Government gave out that he had committed suicide, but the Catholics, with good reason, believed that he had died from the effects of the brutal violence to which he had been subjected.

In contrast to the cruelty shown to Fawkes, Thomas Winter, Oldcorne, and to those of the baser sort, Father Garnet was treated with a certain consideration. The Government, as a matter of policy, clearly wanted to be able to claim in reporting the matter to foreign Powers that he had only been condemned after the fullest enquiry and in a public trial conducted with much parade of the forms of law. King James himself was present on the occasion, as were also the most influential members of the House of Peers. Great deliberation had marked all the proceedings in Garnet's case. Though he had been captured on January 30th, he was only brought to trial on March 28th, and the sentence of death was not carried out until May 3rd. There can be no doubt that during all this period the law officers of the Crown were seeking to obtain evidence against him which would be more convincing than what they were ultimately able to print for the edification of foreign countries in *A True and Perfect Relation*.[1] For a long time there was no proof at all that he had knowledge of the plot beyond the fact that he had been

---

[1] This was translated into Latin and widely circulated on the Continent.

The discovery of Garnet and Oldcorne at Hendlip, from 'Guy Fawkes: or, the Gunpowder Treason' by William Harrison Ainsworth, illustrated by George Cruikshank

intimate with several of the conspirators, and had received a letter from Catesby when he and the rest were attempting to make desperate resistance after the discovery. To the very last it remained true, as Cecil had written on December 4th, that the conspirators, servants, and others who were examined, "obstinately refuse to be accusers of them (the Jesuits), yea, what torture soever they be put to." It was only when Father Garnet had been for some time in confinement that his jailers at last bethought them of a device—the sort of trick that was common enough according to the crooked methods of justice prevalent in those days—by which Garnet and Oldcorne were allowed to converse, believing themselves alone and able to make their confession to each other in the sacrament of penance. Two witnesses were, however, hidden in a secret recess who overheard, though it is admitted very imperfectly, what passed between them. Further, Father Garnet was told that Greenway had been captured, and he was encouraged to write to him, and he was also deceived into thinking that he could communicate safely with Anne Vaux and other friends outside, not knowing that all his letters were intercepted and copied. When challenged with his knowledge of Catesby's plans, which he had avowed to Oldcorne, he at first, and quite justifiably, denied the fact, but when confronted with the eavesdroppers he saw that further concealment would be useless, and in all subsequent examinations there is every reason to suppose that he spoke with absolute sincerity, laying his whole conscience bare. From the disclosures thus made we learn the following facts.

In the summer of 1605 some of the conspirators who had been won over by the persuasions of Catesby began to manifest doubts as to the lawfulness of their design. There were several Catholic peers in the House of Lords, and the Ambassadors of France, Spain, and other Catholic Powers would be present at the opening of Parliament, when the explosion was to take place. They hesitated, accordingly, to involve those whom they considered innocent in common ruin with their enemies. To silence their scruples, Catesby had recourse to a trick. He went to Father Garnet, the superior of the English Jesuits, to whom he was well known, and said he wished to consult him on a point of conscience. He had obtained permission, he said, to pass over to Flanders, and there take service in the army of the Archduke, then at war with the revolted Netherlanders. In the course of the military operations in which he would be engaged, it would, he knew, frequently be necessary, as in the bombardment of a town, to perform operations which would result in killing innocent women and children along with armed soldiers and rebels. Could he with a safe conscience, he asked, participate in such operations? Garnet replied that, according to the divines of every communion, he might in such cases do as he was commanded, such calamities being inseparable from war, and, if wars were therefore to be forbidden, no State would have the power of self-defence if wrongfully attacked. This reply Catesby turned to his own purposes, assuring his confederates, on Garnet's authority, that they need not hesitate because of the sacrifice of some innocent lives.

Although the design was kept profoundly secret, Garnet subsequently began to suspect from the demeanour of Catesby, and expressions which he let fall, that he was projecting some sort of violence against the State, a thing not improbable, for Catesby was a turbulent man who had frequently been engaged in such enterprises on previous occasions. This suspicion filled Garnet with much apprehension and anxiety. On the one hand, he had been strictly commanded by his superiors in Rome to do all in his power to prevent Catholics from resorting to violence, and had, as he tells us, already upon four occasions appeased threatening tumults. On the other hand, he wished, if possible, to avoid the necessity of sacrificing Catesby, who was one of the Catholics committed to his care, and one whom he believed to be warmly attached to himself, though it has been doubted whether he was as trustworthy as Garnet supposed. Having extorted from him a promise that he would do nothing till Rome had been consulted as to the lawfulness of resisting by force the aggression of the Government, Garnet imagined that he had secured tranquillity, for he knew from his own instructions how sternly any such resistance would be forbidden; moreover, he himself wrote to Rome, begging for a still more stringent prohibition of all attempted violence, even under ecclesiastical censures.

His own conduct in this respect he afterwards severely blamed. When he was told what was the real nature of Catesby's design, and how nearly it had succeeded, he thought that he ought to have communicated to the Government his former suspicions, although the King's Ministers would not have been satisfied with guarding against the danger, but would have sought to force him and others, even by torture, to reveal the persons concerned. It was on this account alone that he spoke of himself as "highly guilty," as having offended God and the King, and given a bad example to Catholics—that is, he thus condemned himself because he had not made known his general surmise that *some* violence was projected, which he believed himself to have found means effectually to hinder.

Of Catesby's actual intention he learnt at a later date, and in a manner which made it impossible for him to make any use of his knowledge. Catesby, at a late period of the conspiracy, in spite of the advice he had given to his accomplices, informed the Jesuit Father Greenway, in confession, of what he was about to do. According to the doctrine of the Catholic Church, any knowledge imparted under seal of confession is sacred and inviolable. The confessor can make no use of it, except with the free and full consent of the person confessing. He may severely blame the latter for his conduct and intentions, and is bound to use every means to turn him from a wicked purpose, denouncing upon him the judgments of God, and declaring that there can be no forgiveness for him unless he abandon his sinful design. But if he remain obdurate the confessor may not divulge his secret in order to obviate a result, however terrible. Greenway assures us in the most solemn manner that he did all in his power to dissuade Catesby from his insane and wicked project. Failing in this, he asked his permission to communicate what he had heard, again under seal of confession, to his superior, Garnet; to which Catesby agreed, as also that if the plot should otherwise become known, or if necessary for his own defence, Garnet might make known what he had heard. Having learnt the terrible secret, in this manner, from Greenway, Garnet was, as he assures us, overwhelmed with affliction. He could not sleep, and constantly prayed to God to avert so fearful a crime. But he was helpless to take any other steps, and it is to be remembered that even the Government of the day never ventured to impute it to him as an offence that he kept inviolate the sacramental seal. They confined themselves to attempts to prove that he knew of the plot otherwise than through confession. This he constantly denied, and of this they were never able to produce evidence.

One point in connection with Garnet is held by many persons absolutely to condemn him, namely, his theory and practice of *Equivocation*. It is therefore necessary to understand what he meant. He maintained, in the first place, that it is against reason and justice to ask a man to bear witness against himself. This is now recognised as a first principle by English law, and a prisoner, however conscious of his guilt, is instructed to plead "not guilty." In those days, however, every effort was made to induce an accused person to incriminate himself, and in the case of Garnet in particular there was, as we have said above, no evidence against him except what could be thus obtained. In these circumstances he openly maintained and acted upon the principle that he might rightly and properly deny anything charged against him, of which he believed his accusers to have no other proof than what they hoped to extract from himself. In the second place, he declared, that although we are bound to give testimony against another person who has committed a real offence, and, especially in case of treason, are obliged to give evidence even without being questioned, yet we are not bound to afford information which will cause an innocent man to be unjustly punished; or, rather, are bound not to afford it. A law, he maintained, which made the true Faith treasonable and subjected its ministers to the punishment of traitors, being contrary to the law of God, was no law, and a judge endeavouring to enforce it forfeited all right to be told the truth.

As to the merits of the doctrine thus laid down, it must be sufficient here to observe that it is maintained in like manner by Englishmen of the highest name, who have not the slightest sympathy with Catholics or Jesuits; as by Bishop Jeremy Taylor (*Works,* xiii. 351-71), John Milton (*Christian Doctrine,* ii., c. 13), Archdeacon Paley (*Works,* iv. 123), and Dr. Johnson (*Boswell,* iv. 277). Relating the story of Anthony Dalaber, one of the early Protestants at Oxford, who, when questioned by the authorities as to the whereabouts of a fellow reformer, told them a falsehood in order to save his friend, Mr. Froude (*History,* ii. 57) warmly vindicates his conduct; and Mr. Charles Kingsley, than whom no one ever professed greater zeal for truth, selects this passage of Mr. Froude's for special commendation (*Miscellanies,* ii. 47).

From the evidence, then, which remains to us, it appears to be certain that thirteen turbulent men alone were found to have been engaged in the conspiracy—that it is a mere calumny to charge their guilt upon their fellow Catholics at home or abroad, who vehemently condemned and repudiated the crime—and that as to Father Garnet, who is constantly represented as having been the arch-conspirator, nothing was ever established, except that he did not disclose his general suspicion that some project was on foot, having, as he thought, secured its abandonment. It is very important to remember that this is all of which he ever accused himself, for false and dishonest versions of his words are frequently given by unscrupulous assailants, making it appear that he said the opposite of what he actually did. The following is the full and correct text of his declaration, which is so often misrepresented:

"I, Henry Garnet, of the Society of Jesus, Priest, do here freely protest before God that I hold the late intention of the powder action to have been altogether unlawful and most horrible, as well in respect of the injury and treason to his Majesty, the Prince, and others that should have been sinfully murdered at that time, as also in respect of infinite other innocents, which should have been present. I also protest that I was ever of opinion that it was unlawful to attempt any violence against the King's majesty and the estate, after he was once received by the realm. Also I acknowledge that I was bound to reveal all knowledge that I had of this or any other treason out of the Sacrament of Confession. And whereas, partly upon hope of prevention, partly for that I would not betray my friend, I did not reveal the *general* knowledge of Mr. Catesby's intention which I had by him, I do acknowledge myself highly guilty, to have offended the King's majesty and estate, and humbly ask of all forgiveness; exhorting all Catholics whatsoever, that they no way build upon my example, but by prayer and otherwise seek the peace of the realm, hoping in his Majesty's merciful disposition, that they shall enjoy their wonted quietness, and not bear the burden of mine or others' defaults or crimes. In testimony whereof I have written this with my own hand.

"HENRY GARNET."

That this was the full extent of his connection with the plot we have the high and certainly impartial testimony of Professor

Gardiner, who tells us that on the scaffold Garnet made the following solemn declaration:

"As to the crime of the powder-treason charged against me, as a dying man, before God, I knew nothing of it save in confession. Robert Catesby, however, told me, but only in vague and general terms, that some attempt would be made for the relief of the Catholic cause; but he mentioned nothing certain or definite."

Mr. Gardiner adds: "In all probability this is the exact truth" (*History*, i. 282).

There is nothing, perhaps, which will more effectually convince the thoughtful reader of the innocence of Father Garnet and the other priests than the failure of the Government to make out a satisfactory case against them. They were at the mercy of a procedure which was unscrupulous in its methods and restrained by no judicial recognition of the rights of the accused. Though it is doubtful whether Father Garnet himself was subjected to any more grievous pressure than the threat of torture, that dire expedient was remorselessly employed in the attempt to obtain from others some positive evidence of Jesuit complicity. Fawkes, by the express instructions of the King, was to be subjected to "the gentler tortours at first, *et sic per gradus ad ima tenditur* [i.e., the ordeal was to proceed by degrees to the uttermost], and so God speede your goode worke." Fawkes's ineffectual attempt to sign his deposition with his full name shows how thoroughly these orders were carried out, and the scurrilous pamphlet which describes his execution more than two months after his first racking mentions that "his body being weak with torture and sickness, he was scarce able to go up the ladder, but with much ado, by the help of the hangman, went high enough to break his neck with the fall."

That Thomas Winter was tortured is at least highly probable. We know that his autograph deposition was delayed for

The execution of Guy Fawkes, from 'Guy Fawkes: or, the Gunpowder Treason' by William Harrison Ainsworth, illustrated by George Cruikshank

some time because his hand was not strong enough to write. He had been wounded in the arm at Holbeach, and this may explain his incapacity, but against this we have Cecil's statement on December 4th that "most of the prisoners" could not be brought to inculpate the priests, "yea, what torture soever they be put to." This must surely mean that others besides Fawkes had been racked, and, if so, who were more likely victims than Winter and Bates?

Father Oldcorne was repeatedly tortured. Not only do his fellow Jesuits positively affirm this, but the fact is borne out by the pitiably tremulous signature to his deposition, which they certainly could not have seen.[1] Father Thomas Strange, S.J., though no shred of evidence connected him with the plot, was also most cruelly handled in the hope of extracting some compromising information. He was not put to death, and lived to the age of 69, but his repeated rackings left him an invalid for the rest of his days.[2] About the torture of humbler people, the lay-brothers and servants, little difficulty was made. In one of Garnet's intercepted "orange-juice" letters, he asks his charitable correspondent to procure beds for three servants, James, John, and Henry, his fellow prisoners, "who have all been tortured." Brother Ralph Ashley, the companion of Father Oldcorne, was, of course, subjected to the same ordeal as his superior. "The trembling signature," says Foley, who prints his two depositions, "gives clear indications of the rack."[3] But the worst case was undoubtedly that of Brother Nicholas Owen, already mentioned,

---

[1] See the facsimiles in the late Father Gerard's book, *What was the Gunpowder Plot?* p. 173. If Father Strange, who was in no way implicated, was tortured repeatedly, Oldcorne would certainly not have been spared. We even have a warrant as late as June, 1608, for the torture of Father Laithwaite. See Historical MSS. Commission, *MSS. of Earl Cowper,* Vol. I., p. 60.

[2] Foley, *Records of the English Province, S.J.,* Vol. IV., pp. 3-7.

[3] *Ibid.,* IV., pp. 268-9

the skilled contriver of priests' hiding-places. A piece of evidence which has only been made available of recent years is contained in a dispatch of the Venetian Ambassador Giustiniani, who on March 13th wrote to his Government as follows (the portion in square brackets is in cipher):

> I ought to add that while the King (James) was talking to me he let fall that last night one of the Jesuits, conscience-stricken for his sins, stabbed himself deeply in the body twice with a knife. When the warders ran up at the noise they found him still alive. He confessed to having taken a share in the plot at the suggestion of his Provincial (Garnet), and now, recognising his crime, he had resolved to kill himself, and so escape the terrible death that overhung him, as he deserved. [Public opinion, however, holds that he died of the tortures inflicted on him, which were so severe that they deprived him not only of his strength, but of the power to move any part of his body, and so they think it unlikely that he should have been able to stab himself in the body, especially with a blunt knife, as they allege. It is thought that as he confessed nothing and is dead, they have hoodwinked the King himself by publishing this account] in order to rouse him and everybody to greater animosity against the Catholics and to make the case blacker against his companion the Provincial.[1]

King James's statement that Brother Owen in his dying agony "confessed to having taken a share in the plot at the suggestion of his Provincial," is not only supremely improbable in itself, but is refuted by the fact that not the least use was made of this alleged confession at Garnet's trial. But if the confession was a

---

[1] *Calendar of State Papers: Venetian,* Vol. X., pp. 327-8.

fiction, is there not every likelihood that the whole story of the suicide was a fabrication also?

Human nature is weak and torture is a terrible corrosive, to use a familiar Elizabethan word, when ruthlessly applied. It is hard to believe that if the conspirators had in any sense been led on by priest or Jesuit to embark on such an adventure, not one dupe should have been found in the bitterness of disillusionment to turn upon the crafty arch-plotter and purchase life and favour by a betrayal of the truth.

Further, we are assured by every careful student of the period that in the criminal procedure of those days the prosecution stuck at nothing when they wanted to secure a conviction. Authorities of the highest name, men like Dr. S. R. Gardiner, Sir James Stephen, Jardine, W. S. Holdsworth, Sir Sidney Lee, etc., freely admit that such trials as those of Essex, Raleigh, and Somerset in all which Coke played the foremost rôle, were a travesty of justice. A distinguished jurist, the late Sir John Macdonnell, has recently drawn an astonishing picture of the brutality of Coke in the Raleigh trial. He tells us, for example, in conclusion:

> I come to the evidence. I use that term for want of a better. But according to our rules there was none. A judge in modern times must have directed the acquittal of the prisoner. No one was called to speak to what he saw or heard. No one was cross-examined except indeed the prisoner. The contents of written documents were spoken of without the originals being produced or their absence explained. Even the judges gave evidence—as it turned out, most important evidence. Confessions by A were admitted as conclusive evidence against B ...

Raleigh pressed a point. "My Lords, I claim to have my accuser brought here face to face to speak. I beseech you, my Lords, let Cobham be sent for ... If you proceed to condemn me by bare inferences, without an oath, without a subscription, without witnesses, upon a paper accusation, you try me by the Spanish inquisition. If my accuser were dead or abroad, it were something; but he liveth and is in this very house." He was unjust to the Spanish inquisition; its procedure would have been more regular and fairer.[1]

One is led to ask, Is it probable that the Jesuits in the then state of public opinion would be more likely to meet with fair play than such high-placed offenders as Essex or Raleigh? Essex and Raleigh, after all, had some powerful sympathisers, but the Jesuits had no friends in England who could exercise the least influence in their behalf, especially at such a moment.

Lastly, although Dr. Gardiner, as we have seen, acquits the Jesuits of any direct participation in the plot, still he finds them blameworthy in this, that "they did not take such measures as were lawful and possible to avert the disaster."[2] But surely we may ask—given the inviolability of confessional knowledge, and the danger of seeming to have used that knowledge if any warning founded on general suspicions had been conveyed to the Government—what means *could* have been devised to avert the disaster? It was a hopeless entanglement for men situated as they were. Had Garnet or any priest gone straight to Cecil, even apart from the risk to himself of arrest, torture, and prolonged imprisonment, he would have been branded by most Catholics, if his intervention had become known, as the most despicable

[1] Sir John Macdonnell, *Historical Trials* (Oxford, Clarendon Press, 1927), pp. 177-9.

[2] *What Gunpowder Plot Was*, p. 199.

of traitors. Other means of prevention, they would have said, ought to have been found. No doubt Garnet himself felt this. He counted on his influence with Catesby and on his appeal to Rome. But communications with Rome were slow, especially for proscribed men. Dr. Gardiner sometimes seems to speak as if Garnet had only to go to the nearest post-office and send a telegram, to get it all settled. On the other hand, Catesby, fascinating as he seems to have been, was a strange man, whose real mind was incalculable.[1] Both Garnet and Greenway appear to have made the mistake of thinking him more trustworthy and docile to authority than he really was. They probably abstained from more violent denunciation of his schemes for fear of alienating him. Peaceful persuasion seemed their only chance. But it was a situation in which whatever they did would, in the light of subsequent events, have been proved a blunder.

Let us imagine—to take an extravagant supposition—that it was Garnet's brain, and not Cecil's or Tresham's, which had conceived the device of sending the warning to Monteagle. It was a scheme which, while ensuring the frustration of the plot, seemed likely to secure such timely warning for the conspirators as would enable them to make their escape. If they had acted upon the news communicated to them by Ward on October 27th-28th concerning the mysterious letter which he had read aloud at Monteagle's table, they might have got away and reached the Continent. The plan may have been kindly meant, but in point of fact it failed. Suppose the plan had been Father Garnet's, could he ever have dared to own himself the author of it? He would have been looked upon as the murderer

---

[1] Nothing is more astounding than the fact that after the discovery of the plot Catesby tried to rally Sir Everard Digby and other sympathisers assembled at Dunchurch by telling them that the King and Cecil were dead and that this was the moment to rise in rebellion. *Calendar of State Papers: Domestic, 1603–1610*, p. 260.

of all the Catholics, some twenty in number (including the chivalrous Sir Everard Digby and his own fellow Jesuits), who lost their lives in consequence. Moreover, all the torture of innocent serving-men, the anguish of wives, the forfeiture of estates, and the discredit to the whole cause would have been laid at his door. Father Garnet, as his letters show, was a man of tender conscience and not lacking in imagination. We may well believe his own statement that in the impasse in which he found himself he could not sleep for trouble of mind, and saw no help in any means but prayer.

Procession of a guy. Taken from 'The Book of Days' (1864), edited by Robert Chambers

Printed in Great Britain
by Amazon